*Expelled from the Garden*

# *Other Works by Sandy Krolick*

# Expelled from the Garden

*Sandy Krolick, Ph.D.*

*Islands Press*
*New York : Altai Krai : Florida*

ISBN: 978-1-7350698-9-0

*Once natural causation has been swept out of the world by doctrines of reward and punishment some sort of un-natural causation becomes necessary: and all other varieties of the denial of nature follow it.*

Friederich Nietzsche, *The Antichrist*

## Expelled from the Garden

While the normal give and take of everyday life oftentimes seems like the Rubik's Cube — a three dimensional puzzle teasing us first one way and then another, attempting to unravel and understand the unquestionably peculiar character of *religious faith* requires a mode of reflection far less familiar and, for that very reason, far more difficult to grasp. Yet, while the task before us is certainly a daunting one, there is absolutely no reason to shy away from the inquiry itself. In fact there is every reason to proceed and, if we are successful, try to unravel the apparent *interiority* and *opacity* of the religious temperament. However, please note that in this current project we do not aim for certitude so much as we simply wish to expose the relative fallacy of the faith experiment, and of Christian faith specifically. Expulsion was just the beginning, and it was an invitation to expose the frailty of faith.

Religion — that customary domain of priest, prophet, and shaman — has been routinely tasked with providing answers to an array of life's most pressing questions and concerns. In fact, it has long been argued that religious faith provides some sort of absolute grounding in the midst of otherwise apparently confusing and seemingly hopeless conditions. Believers typically pursue the comfort that faith provides insofar as it helps them to deal more effectively, if not more easily, with the visceral challenges of existential unpredictability.

But does faith really help overcome such uncertainties, or does it simply mask the underlying and discomforting perception of meaninglessness with some fantastic expectations and a promise of final salvation? Can faith in some divine figure satisfactorily address the trauma, the feelings of abandonment, or the often uncanny sense of being ill-at-ease in the world? Does faith in some divine plan provide concrete assistance to the oddball, the misbegotten, or those who are simply outcast? Does faith even offer legitimate cover for those of us considered to be well-adjusted? These are just some preliminary questions. Yet, those among of us who have spent years reading through any number of tomes seeking answers to such questions have found themselves strewn across the muddied ground of history or lying face down on the broken bones of ancient but apparently well-intentioned philosophers.

Then perhaps we should abandon all those well-worn and tired expressions we hear from the true believers, ignore their forgiveness of our sins, and give up laboring under the illusion that we can somehow realize an otherworldly satisfaction, some spiritual reward in an afterlife or some other exalted heavenly state. Indeed, it may be a more fruitful tactic simply to call out this spiritual craving for what it really appears to be — a phantom, a fake, a figment of some wishful imaginings. Actually, this religious temperament itself appears to be no more than "fruit from a poisonous tree" — just another consequence of that bite from the forbidden apple in Big Daddy's garden. And, while the serpent may have taken the principal blame, it was Adam who suffered the consequences along with his tempting seductress, Eve, both of whom were then unceremoniously cast out of paradise — naked and displaced — now saddled with the unwanted and unforgiving knowledge of 'good' and 'evil'. But, as we find with this Old Testament tale, deception was and remains the name of the game that religion relies upon in first corralling and then fleecing its flock.

So what path remains open to us? What avenue of inquiry may we legitimately pursue at this current juncture in our reflections? Is there some concrete approach that will place us on a more secure trajectory or help us divine an answer? Or is it just the case that such questions can never be answered satisfactorily; that there are no terms to provide lasting comfort, no real transcendental options available, no salvific *deus ex machina*?

In attempting to address such questions as these, let us turn attention to what I would consider some preliminary issues or first principles. This is the question we must ask before all others: Is our current historical posture, our faith in some transcendent God, absolutely primal or essential to human life? Let us explore this briefly. If we glance back — far back into the misty origins of our species — we find that our earliest forebear, *Homo erectus,* roamed the earth approximately two million years ago. Our own species, *Homo sapiens* — or anatomically modern humans — emerged on scene roughly three hundred thousand years ago. But the earliest evidence of any religious or proto-religious activity in human prehistory emerged with some certainty only around fifty-thousand years ago, during what we call the Upper Paleolithic period. It was at this point that we see the first real signs of religious-like or shamanic ritual practices. And our evidence for such practices may be deduced from examining pieces of Paleolithic art, including cave painting and Venus figurines.

*Homo sapiens*, then, does not appear to be a religious creature by nature. Rather, we human beings have acquired our faith and our faithfulness much like we have come by any number of other cultural tools and traditions — through centuries if not millennia of social transmission, training, experimentation, and adaptation. In fact, historically we have allowed select members of society and, more recently, the collective memory of one person above all others — the one who was hung from a cross — to stitch together an overarching narrative addressing the entire set of events leading up to the phenomenon of Christian faith today. Yet, this story did not really explode across the screen until many millennia after our species first walked the earth, and long after the rise of the earliest civilizations along the Fertile Crescent in the Ancient Near East roughly four-thousand years before the current era.

Be that as it may, we find that an increasingly overwhelming number of our compatriots have grown accustom to belief in some transcendent, magnificent, and all-powerful Being hovering somewhere not too far above the clouds, the One who enlivens us as well as providing us with some meaning and justification beyond this world of everyday experience. But, is it really required that life have some ultimate purpose, some divinely crafted sense above what we give to it or experience everyday? Is there some underlying reason or necessity for belief in an all-knowing, celestial presence that is guiding us? Or is the supernatural just a creation of someone with a cudgel (or a cross) leading us around by the nose, someone we follow unthinkingly out of an uncanny sense of fear and trembling?

Unfortunately, the multitudes are still wandering around in the dark, eyes closed, unable or perhaps unwilling to recognize their own strength — that primal energy driving each and every one of us from within. Yet, it is this very power, that feral core lodged somewhere within our genetic makeup, confirming that we alone are the prime movers and the final arbiters, that we alone define truth and falsehood, good and evil, just as we were condemned to do so ever since being cast out of that mythical garden. It is now — and has always been — both our birthright and our ontological obligation to define our personal values through the choices we make and the actions we take. As the philosopher reminds us:

> *Let us not underestimate this fact: that we*
> *ourselves, we free spirits, are already a*
> *'transvaluation of all values,' a visualized*
> *declaration of war and victory against all*
> *the old concepts of 'true' and 'not*
> *true.' (Antichrist, 13)*

But, what exactly is Nietzsche referring to here? What does he mean when he speaks about a *transvaluation* of values? The statement seems to suggest that, in following the paths recommended and taken by those ancient 'scribes' and 'wise men', we have effectively gone down the wrong road from the very dawn of history, the very beginning, only to realize that we have been ensnared in a trap of our own devising, exalting suffering instead of strength, weakness instead of power. Are we not here and now put on notice concerning our own accountability in this matter — that we are the creators of value, that we determine right from wrong, truth from falsehood, good from evil — as the story in Genesis clearly and unapologetically reminds us? Is there no longer a divine mandate, no absolute celestial judgement or commandments to be handed down? If not, then allowing the free reign to our basic impulses must be a fundamental right as well as our principal obligation. This is a return to origins, to the primal, to the organic, to that which is essentially human — before the birth of civilization, and prior to the religious hijacking of the concepts of 'good' and 'evil'. But, 'What is good?' asks Nietzsche. And his answer:

> *Whatever augments the feeling of power, the will to power, power itself, in man. (Antichrist, 2)*

Here we are brought directly and concretely face to face with the experience of primeval power, a manifestation of that vital force buried deep within the folds of our flesh, our natural capacity or *pouvoir* — our ability to reach out, to touch, to move, and engage the world.

Much more than a mere physical presence within the world, my own corporeity demonstrates a motility, a motor intentionality. From the simple positioning of my body, whether passively suffering or forcefully acting, my flesh expresses its natural reflexivity, turning back upon itself, both the breach and bridge that constitute my being-situated within a world. This somatic facing in two directions — inward (proprioceptive), and outward (tactile) — reflects the real ground of my being concretely situated.

Meanwhile, the Christian faith only serves to increase our sense of despair, making us more enfeebled, tamed, and civilized, constantly working to neuter or destroy that primal passion and instinct that motivates, drives, and feeds us. Such faith does not serve to enhance that fundamental experience of power, but rather it rejoices in our suffering, elevating weakness and adversity as we see in the crucifixion of its well-mythologized salvific hero. To be a Christian is to be grateful for the suffering, and thankful that HE has already been crucified for our sake — *died for our sins*. Such faith reveals a much deeper, more penetrating loss: that we have become subject to an otherworldly phantom, a tyranny that must be stopped. We must allow no safe harbor for the Christian idea of sin to rot us from within as we are told to wait patiently for the big finale — *The Rapture*.

If, in fact, our actions arise organically — from the 'beasts' of the field as it were — then there really is no place here for any moral condemnation. The God of Christian faith has simply become a torment, a plague against our fundamental nature. Once we admit this openly, we can leave the hall of mirrors that serves only to confuse and confound us. We need to understand that we are part of the flesh of this world, that we live inexorably within the folds of that flesh — where our own *interiority* comes out to touch the world and where the world, in turn, reaches in to touch us — whether we like it or not, whether the breeze is pleasant or cold. Still, we must learn to enjoy the taste of blood on our tongues and the feel of dirt between our toes. We are, after all, just human… all too human!